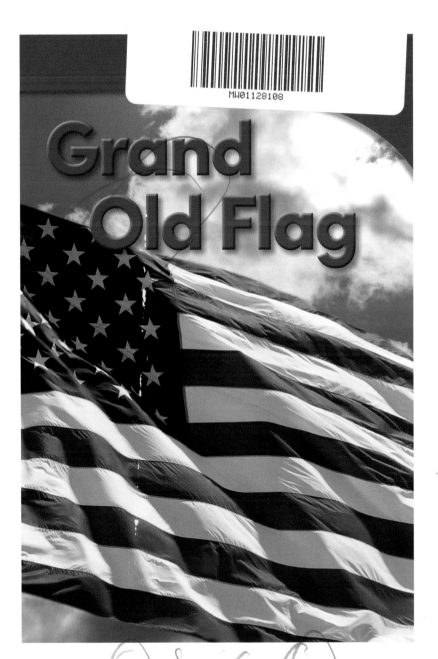

Grand Old Flag

Dona Herweck Rice

Publishing Credits

Rachelle Cracchiolo, M.S.Ed., *Publisher*
Conni Medina, M.A.Ed., *Managing Editor*
Jamey Acosta, *Content Director*
Dona Herweck Rice, *Series Developer*
Robin Erickson, *Multimedia Designer*

Image Credits: pp. 3, 5, 6, 7, 12 ©Kristoffer Tripplaar/Alamy; p.4 ©iStock.com/studo58; pp. 8-9
©Dennis Macdonald/Alamy; p.11 ©iStock.com/Jani Bryson; all other images from Shutterstock.

Library of Congress Cataloging-in-Publication Data

Library of Congress Control Number: 2015938707

Teacher Created Materials

5301 Oceanus Drive
Huntington Beach, CA 92649-1030
http://www.tcmpub.com

ISBN 978-1-4938-2055-9

© 2016 Teacher Created Materials, Inc.
Printed in China
Nordica.122018.CA21801437

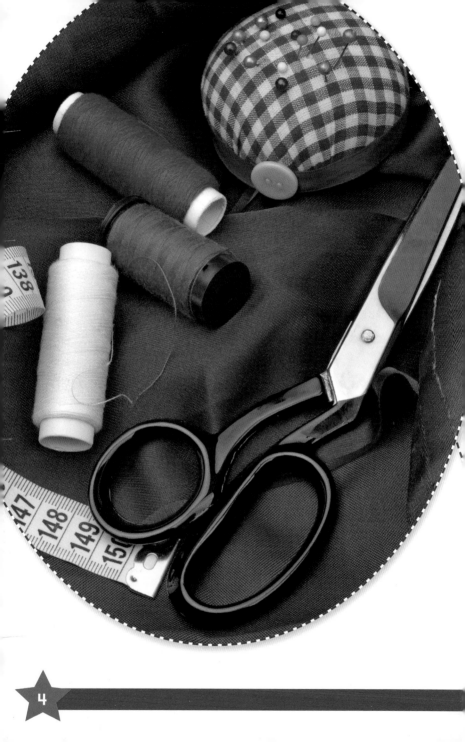

8

Words to Know

flag

sew

stars

stripes